Cross Training

Top 100 Cross Training WOD's with Pictures!

Dan Smith

Table of Contents

Introduction

I want to thank you and congratulate you for purchasing this book…

"Top 100 Cross Training WOD's with Pictures!"

Cross Training is an effective and innovative way to shape up and improve your overall physical health. Greg Glassman and Lauren Jenai established this in 2000.

Cross Training is not just any other workout fad. It was developed to be a physical philosophy, merging many different sports, disciplines and movements in the course of their workouts. The benefits of Cross Training have gained much popularity over the years, and now this exercise is being practiced in thousands of gyms all around the world.

Cross Training is targeted to all people of all sexes and of all body types, and there is always a workout routine that can suit your exercise needs. Whether it is to lose weight, to shape up or bulk up, Cross Training is never a routine based workout. Every day is different, and with the right equipment and proper knowledge of how to do the exercises, you can do Cross Training just about anywhere, even if you don't have all the time to show up at the gym.

Many people look to Cross Training as their key to an attractive and healthy body. It is very convenient, especially for people with busy schedules. Cross Training gives you the maximum amount of calories burned in a short period of time. Your workouts will be short, but intense, lasting at around 20 to 30 minutes and can be customized according to what you need, and what you want to do.

This book will give you access to many of the Cross Training workouts you can do every day. The exercises here are geared toward all kinds of people with different body types: men, women, as well as for the people who either want to get lean or bulk up or to just simply look great in general.

Working out isn't just about the way you look. It is about maintaining a healthy and well-functioning body. This calorie blasting workout book is also packed with cardio, flexibility and endurance boosting exercises. Along with the workout descriptions will be pictures to you get a good idea on how executing a particular workout will look like.

The exercises here and short and challenging, and the key to getting through them is your determination to push through and succeed. If these workouts are done diligently and properly, you may just be able to see and feel the results in no time, and no wonder why so many people are hooked on Cross Training already.

Thanks again for purchasing this book,

I hope you enjoy it!

How to Keep Yourself Safe from Cross Training Related Injuries

Since Cross Training was developed from so many other types of discipline, you can expect your usual injuries to be almost the same as the ones you can get from gymnastics, power lifting and weight lifting, if you are not careful enough. It is advised that beginners try Cross Training in a gym with a trainer who can guide you on how to position your body properly.

Even the more experienced ones in Cross Training should always observe the proper positioning of your joints and limbs. Never do shortcuts with your movements, even if it feels easier. It will lessen your risk of injury.

If you feel that you have not gained enough experience in Cross Training yet, it may be better to either keep going to the gym first, with a certified trainer, or do the less intense workouts while doing them at home. Watching videos on Cross Training can also give you a good idea on how to prevent any injuries.

Warming your body up before engaging in any high intensity sport is important. Do not attempt to do your workouts if you feel like your body is not prepared for it yet. Stretching will be a good way to start along with some easy cardio.

Chapter 1: Workout of the Day Cross Training exercises for the Beginner

These exercises can help you get the hang of Cross Training without over exerting your body. These are not just for beginners though; these are also great for individuals who may want a less intense workout for the day. These workouts, as most Cross Training workouts, are AMRAP. You can set your own pace and do as many repetitions you like.

www.wallpaperup.com

1. Cross Training Workout of the Day For Beginners #1: Sit-Ups and Lunges

Estimated time is 8 minutes with 3 minutes allotted for Sit-Ups, 3 minutes for lunges and two minutes for rest. You are supposed to push yourself to your limit within the three minutes of sit ups and lunges, doing fifteen of each in the allotted time frame. The two minutes is meant for you to recover, but the two minutes will not be enough for you to get comfortable. If you are beginning to find this one a bit too easy, even after a few repetitions, you are welcome to add weights to your lunges to make it all the more challenging.

www.wallpaperup.cm

2. *Cross Training WOD for Beginners #2: The Half Cindy*

The Full Cindy takes twice the time you will need for the Half Cindy, which is 10 minutes. For this workout, you will need to do 5 pull ups, 10 push ups and 15 air squats within the allotted time frame. Do these for a few rounds and do not forget to keep track of how many you've done. For people who cannot do full push ups, they may substitute with doing push ups on their knees or on a chair. For people who want more of a challenge, resistance bands and weights can be used.

i.ytimg.com

3. Cross Training WOD for Beginners # 3: Burpees and Wall Ball

You will have to do your burpees and wall ball in reps of 21, 15 and 9, according to your own time. Though it is good to take some rest in between, you might like to go on with your burpees to make this workout easier to get through. You will need a ball for this particular exercise.

www.wallpaperup.com

4. *Cross Training WOD for Beginners #4: Helen*

Helen will take you three rounds, and to your own speed. This is a running workout, and you are advised to know your body's limits while doing this workout. This will be a 400-meter run, 21 American kettle- bell swings, and 12 pull ups. You may also substitute the swings with another suitable exercise if these are still too hard to accomplish.

www.wallpaperup.com

5. Cross Training WOD for Beginners #5: The Cross Training Total

For this, you may find yourself with a bit of heavy lifting to help start building up your strength. You will have to do 5 back squats, 3 overhead presses, and 3 deadlifts to complete this workout, and AMRAP. This workout will need complete attention to your form to minimize any risk for injury. This one will be easier done if you know how to execute these properly; you can also do these with your trainer. Though AMRAP still applies to this exercise you should know your limits and do only what your body can handle.

www.wallpaperup.com

6. *Cross Training WOD for Beginners #6: Burpee Box Jumps*

The Burpee Box Jumps are done as an AMRAP exercise. To begin you must 8 box jumps. To execute this, you must stay in front of the box while performing a burpee, followed by jumping up to the box.

i.ytimg.com

7. Cross Training WOD for Beginners #7: The Squat Routine

Basically you spend two minutes in a squat position as you perform this WOD. Then you follow up with ten burpees, fifteen sit ups and 20 air squats, and continue doing this for 2 more rounds.

www.wikihow.com

8. *Cross Training WOD for Beginners #8: Lunges and Jumps*

You're going to have to do 15 lunges with your dumbbells, followed by 60 double unders with a jump rope, to complete this WOD. Repeat this for a total of five rounds, in your best time.

www.bodbot.com

9.   *Cross Training WOD for Beginners #9: The Farmer's Workout*

You are going to need a jump rope and some light dumbbells for this exercise. Go on your jump rope for three minutes, doing either singles or double unders. After that, take your dumbbells and do you weighted sit ups. You must also be consistent enough to reach three minutes. To complete the whole WOD, follow up with farmers carry lunges, with your dumbbells still in your hand. You are allowed a minute rest in between each exercise.

www.wallpaperup.com

10. Cross Training WOD for Beginners #10: Front Squats and Run

Your workout of the Day will consist of 12 front squats, 10 pull ups, 8 push presses followed by a 400 meter run. Do three rounds to finish.

www.vigourandvitality.wordpress.com

11. Cross Training WOD for Beginners #11: Tabata Mash Up

The mash up is done in 20 seconds movements with a 10 second resting time. First you do push-ups and then you follow up with alternating lunges. Keep doing these movements until you reach a total of eight minutes.

www.wallpaperup.com

12. Cross Training WOD for Beginners #12: The Ten Minute Swing Jump and Dip

This workout will last you a total of ten minutes. You will have to do 10 kettle bell swings, 10 box jumps, and 10 ring dips to have your WOD fix.

www.wallpaperup.com

13. *Cross Training WOD for Beginners #13: Countdown*

The Countdown is actually a countdown for your reps. Start with ten, then 9, then eight, until you reach 1. To do this WOD, you must do dumbbell thrusters and kettle bell swings.

www.active.sweatband.com

14. *Cross Training WOD for Beginners #14: Use Your Body Weight*

This exercise will require you nothing but the use of your body weight. This may seem easy enough, but your full weight is actually quite enough to develop a good physique. 10 push-ups, 10 air squats, 10 ring rows, 15 sit ups and 5 burpees will be enough for this WOD.

i.ytimg.com

15. Cross Training WOD for Beginners #15: The 530 Meter Sandwich

This is a definitive challenge for the Cross Training beginners. You will have to do a 530 meter run at the start and the end of this route. In between, do 40 air squats 30 sit ups 20 burpees and 10 pull ups.

www.wallpaperup.com

These exercises will help you get the hang of how Cross Training works. These are also perfect for people who are travelling or exercising at home. You can amp up the challenges by doing more repetitions or adding more weights. These exercises aren't necessarily for be- ginners only. These can build your strength, endurance, agility and stamina.

Chapter 2: The Cross Training Girls

The "Girls" Workout of Day is mainly a series of challenging movements still done without much use of heavy equipment. These, as the name suggests, are quite suitable for women, though are actually the original Cross Training benchmark exercises given to males and females alike. But these WODs are quite effective and challenging, and some- times downright exhausting, and all Cross Training athletes wanting to get whipped up to shape should do this. These Girls burn calories and build muscle like no other, and they can get you closer to your ideal body in very little time.

16. *Cross Training Girls WOD #1: Annie*

Annie lets you do this workout in intervals of 50- 40- 30- 20- 10. The exercise will require you to do Double Unders and Sit ups. You may want to include a jump rope for this exercise.

www.fitnessmag.co.za

17. *Cross Training Girls WOD #2: Barbara*

Barbara is not the usual ladies' fare. Barbara defines your muscles like no other with 20 pull ups, 30 push-ups, 40 sit ups and 50 squats. Challenge yourself to five rounds to complete this Workout of the Day.

www.Cross Trainingoneworld.typepad.com

18. *Cross Training Girls WOD #3: Cindy*

You have met Half Cindy in the Beginning of this eBook. Now it is time to meet the full Cindy. To do this WOD, begin with 10 pull ups, and then go down to 15 push ups. Complete this workout with 15 squats. This is an AMRAP workout to be done the course of twenty minutes.

19. *Cross Training Girls WOD #4: Chelsea*

Chelsea is a thirty minute Workout of the Day. You will be doing 5 pull ups, 10 push ups and 10 squats, and you can to the repetitions to your own speed. This is a lighter but still challenging WOD.

www.wallpaperup.com

20. *Cross Training Girls WOD #5: Angie*

Angie is the ultimate competition. You will have to get past a hundred pull ups, a hundred push ups, one hundred sit ups and one hundred squats to get through this Workout of the Day.

g-ecx.images-amazon.com

21. *Cross Training Girls WOD #6: Eva*

Eva will need you to do an 800 meter run. After that, you'll have to do 30 kettlebell swings, and 30 pull ups. Eva is a test of strength and endurance.

www.wallpaperswide.com

22. *Cross Training Girls WOD #7: Amanda*

Amanda is all for the heavy lifting. You will need a weight of at least 135 pounds for 9- 7- 5 intervals of Muscle Ups and Snatch.

23. *Cross Training Girls WOD #8: Karen*

This Workout of the Day will require you to perform 150 wall balls.

d2ufjv2mjmrw7m.cloudfront.com

24. *Cross Training Girls WOD #9: Mary*

Mary is an AMRAP workout that includes five handstand push ups, ten single-leg squats, and fifteen pull ups. Do as many as you can.

www.google.co.in

25. *Cross Training Girls WOD #10: Nicole*

Nicole is an AMRAP Workout that needs you to do a 400 meter run, and your maximum number of pull ups.

starportwellness.files.wordpress.com

26. Cross Training Girls WOD # 11: Kelly

Kelly is also a 400 meter run, like Nicole, but with the pull ups substituted with 30 box jumps and thirty wall balls repeated for five rounds, giving you a much different kind of burn from the Nicole.

27. *Cross Training Girls WOD # 12: Diane*

The 225 pound deadlift makes Diane for the heavy lifters. To do this WOD, do deadlifts and handstand push ups on the interval of 21, 15 and 9.

www.wallpaperup.com

28. *Cross Training Girls WOD # 13: Fran*

To complete the Fran WOD, you must do Thrusters and pull ups in the intervals of 21, 15 and 9.

29. *Cross Training Girls WOD # 14: Elizabeth*

Elizabeth is another 21- 15- 9 interval WOD. You will have to execute Cleans and ring dips, and you will have to carry the weight of 135 lbs.

www.google.co.in

30. Cross Training Girls WOD #15: Nancy

Nancy is a WOD done in five rounds. First you must do a four hundred meter run. Then do fifteen overhead squats with a 95 pound total weight.

www.wallpaperup.com

31. *Cross Training Girls WOD #16: Helen*

Helen is a mix of a four hundred meter run, 21 kettlebell swings and 12 pull ups. You should repeat these for three rounds.

www.watchfit.com

32. Cross Training Girls WOD #17 Lynne

Lynne is quite the strength booster. Do your maximum counts of body weight bench presses and pull ups, and do this for five rounds.

Previews.123rf.com

Chapter 3: Cross Training WOD's Without Equipment

The following exercises can all be done without equipment. This is perfect for the people who have no access to a gym, or are currently away from any access to weights, exercise balls and the like.

33. Cross Training WOD without Equipment #1: The Susan

The Susan should consist of 5 reps, done for time. Taking your time can help you track your progress in Cross Training. Start this exercise with a 200 meter run, followed by ten squats, and finished off with 10 push ups. Repeat as needed. The Susan is also part of the original Cross Training Girls workout.

www.losingweightdone.com

34. *Cross Training WOD without Equipment #2: Jackknives*

True to its name, this workout is all jackknives. You will start with 10 jackknife handstands to a vertical to a vertical jump, another ten handstand jackknives to a tuck jump, and then another ten handstand jackknives to a straddle jump.

www.bodbot.com

35. *Cross Training WOD without Equipment #3: The L sits*

You will have to do ten rounds of this workout. You will have to exe- cute ten L sits off the floor then repeat.

i.yitmg.com

36. Cross Training WOD without Equipment #4: Rounds: 10 Push Ups and Squats

This exercise will need you to accomplish 10 rounds of ten push ups and ten squats. The many repetitions will help you build muscle and help you firm up your body.

www.gqindia.com

37. Cross Training WOD without Equipment #5: Handstand Push Ups + 200 Meter Run

This exercise is done for time. You will have to execute 10 Handstand Push Ups, followed by a 200 meter run. You will have to repeat this exercise thrice.

d2ufjv2mjmrw7m.cloudfront.net

38. Cross Training WOD without Equipment #6: One Mile and A Minute

This one can be done to your own time as you complete a one mile run. After every one minute of your run, you will have to complete a mini workout consisting of 10 air squats, 10 push ups, and 10 sit ups.

39. Cross Training WOD without Equipment #7: Push Ups, Air Squats and Sit Ups

This is very much like the previous exercise, but without the one mile run. Do ten push ups, ten air squats, and 10 sit ups and do six repetitions of this whole routine.

www.wallpaperup.com

40. *Cross Training WOD without Equipment #8: Push Ups, Air Squats and Sit Ups*

This involves the Push Up, Air Squat and Sit Up Trio too. All three of these are still done by tens; only this time, ten repetitions of this routine will be needed. This is a bigger challenge compared to the previous routine.

www.wallpaperup.com

41. Cross Training WOD without Equipment #9: Push Ups and Dash

You will have to do 10 push ups and a hundred-meter dash to complete one repetition. This exercise requires you to accomplish ten full repetitions to complete, and you can do this according to your own time.

www.wallpaperup.com

42. *Cross Training WOD without Equipment #10: Run with Push Ups and Hollow Rocks*

This is another running exercise, requiring you to complete a 200 meter run, followed by ten push ups and ten hollow rocks. You will have to complete ten rounds of this exercise. This is great for cardio and strength building and endurance.

43. Cross Training WOD without Equipment #11: Sit Ups and Burpees

This is a great core exercise for your next Workout of the Day. To do this, do ten rounds of ten sit ups and ten burpees.

44. Cross Training WOD without Equipment #12: Hand Release Push Ups, V Sits and Squats

This is a great full body workout for anyone to do. Start with 10 Hand release push ups, 10 V Sits and ten squats. You will need to do ten rounds in your own time, though you may lessen according to your own personal limit. Remember to record this to keep track of your Cross Training progress.

i.ytimg.com

45. Cross Training WOD without Equipment #13: Run with Vertical Jumps

This workout of the day requires you to complete a 400 meter run along followed by 10 vertical jumps, done to your own record time. To complete this workout, you will need to do a total of 5 rounds.

46. i.ytimg.comCross Training WOD without Equipment #14: Vertical Jumps with Push Ups and Sit Ups

The Vertical Jumps amp up this full body workout by adding some cardio to strength building and core exercises. To complete this Workout of the Day, do ten vertical jumps, with 10 push ups and ten sit ups. Do this to your own pace, record your time and repeat for a total of four rounds.

47. Cross Training WOD without Equipment #15: Walking Lunges and Push Ups

The walking lunges and push ups may seem relatively easy to do, but the challenge here lies in the amount of rounds you have to complete. Do ten walking lunges and ten push-ups for time. Repeat for ten rounds.

www.lukehealthfitness.com

48. Cross Training WOD without Equipment #16: The One Hundred Meter Dash

This Workout of the Day will end up testing your endurance and speed. To do this workout you will have to run 100 meters, according to your own best time. You will then have to do another ten rounds of these, all while catching the time it took you on your first run on every run.

wallpaperwide.com

49. Cross Training WOD without Equipment #17: A Hundred Air Squats

This Workout of the Day will be all air squats, and will be great for firming up. Complete one hundred air squats according to your own time. Allow yourself three minutes of resting time, and then repeat until you reach a total of three rounds.

50. Cross Training WOD without Equipment #18: Air Squat AMRAP Challenge

Beat your best time. Complete 100 Air Squats. This is great cardio and can help you shape up from the many repetitions. This is also great for people who can accomplish the previous Air Squat WOD with no problem.

www.kellyprincewrites.com

51. Cross Training WOD without Equipment # 19: Burpee AMRAP Challenge

Complete 100 Burpees. You may do as many repetitions as you find fit. The many repetitions will help you build your desired muscle tone.

i.ytimg.com

52. *Cross Training WOD without Equipment # 20: 100 Push Ups*

This an ultimate test of upper body strength. You can only complete this workout if you can accomplish the 100 push ups.

www.reddeltaproject.com

53. *Cross Training WOD without Equipment # 21: 100- 75- 50- 25*

This workout of the day is a full body workout consisting of cardio, strength building, and agility. DO a hundred jumping jacks, followed by 75 air squats, 50 push ups and 25 burpies. You can do this workout according to your own time. This is a great workout to build up some sweat.

media3.popsugar-assets.com

54. *Cross Training WOD without Equipment # 22: Burpies and Sit Ups 10 to 1 ladder*

Do the Burpees and Sit Ups in a 10 to 1 interval.

thumbs.dreamstime.com

55. Cross Training WOD without Equipment # 23: Sit Ups with 100 meter sprint 10 to 1 ladder

Do a hundred meter sprint and follow it up with sit ups.

i.ytimg.com

56. *Cross Training WOD without Equipment #24: Push Ups with 100 meter sprint 10 to 1 ladder*

Do the push ups after sprinting a hundred meters and keep count of the intervals.

i.ytimg.com

57. Cross Training WOD without Equipment #25: 30 Second Handstand and Squat

Execute and hold a handstand for thirty seconds. After the handstand hold the bottom of your squat for another thirty seconds. Repeat this until you complete the required 10 sets.

knowledge.freeletics.com

58. Cross Training WOD without Equipment #26: Ten 50 Meter Sprints

This WOD will need you to complete ten 50 meter sprints with only 2 minutes of rest in between sprints. This will be a challenge for your own personal speed and endurance.

www.hdwalpaperscool.com

59. Cross Training WOD without Equipment #27: For Time: Jacks, Burpies, and Squats

You will have to do this Workout of the Day for time. Complete twenty jumping jacks, followed by 20 burpies and twenty squats and repeat the exercises thrice.

i.huffpost.com

60. Cross Training WOD without Equipment #28: For Time: Sit Ups, Push Ups and a 400-meter run

This WOD will require at least four repetitions. You have to execute 20 sit ups and 20 push ups followed by a 400 meter run to get that full body burn.

61. Cross Training WOD without Equipment #29: Vertical Jumps, Long Jumps and Squats

This is a fast WOD concentrated on firming and strengthening the legs. Complete three vertical jumps, three squats, and three long jumps. You need to do five rounds of that.

image.shutterstock.com

62.   Cross Training WOD without Equipment #30: Tuck Jumps and Handstands

Accomplish three rounds of twenty tuck jumps followed by another three rounds of holding your handstand. The handstand is a great exercise for improving your balance.

s-media-cache-ak0.pinimg.com

63. Cross Training WOD without Equipment #31: Exercise for Technique and Form

Cross Training is actually a great full body workout for just about anyone because you can work with no equipment with just your body weight. To do this WOD, do five handstands into a jackknife to a high jump. Follow this with another five handstands, jackknife to tuck jump, and completed by five handstands, jackknife to split jump. Do three rounds of this.

cdn.sheknows.com

64. *Cross Training WOD without Equipment # 32: Push Ups With Plank*

Do 10 rounds of five push ups followed by a plank, which is hold- ing the top part of your push up while holding the rest of your body straight for half a minute. This exercise is great for your upper body and core.

www.wikihow.com

65. Cross Training WOD without Equipment #33: Squat and Burpie Seven

The execution is simple. Do seven squats and seven burpies, and do this for seven rounds. This is one of the shorter Cross Training WODs, which can also easily be done by beginners.

media.gettyimages.com

66. Cross Training WOD without Equipment # 34: Push Up to Burpie

Do ten push ups and stretch yourself out to a burpee. You should do this for at least five rounds.

tonygentilcore.com

67. Cross Training WOD without Equipment #35: Squats with Breathing

To do this Cross Training WOD, perform one squat, hold at the bottom, and then take one breath. Follow this with two squats, and while holding the squat, take two breaths. Do this up to ten and repeat as much as you can. This is an AMRAP exercise. These can also be done with weights if you want a more intense workout.

i.ytimg.com

68. *Cross Training WOD without Equipment # 36: The Invisible Fran*

The Invisible Fran will have you follow a 21- 15- 9 scheme of repetitions while doing air squats and push ups. This WOD is done for time.

www.wallpaperup.com

69. Cross Training WOD without Equipment # 37: Plebs Plank +Squat and Hollow Rock Hold

This workout is all about having the strength to hold yourself into position. This exercise will consist of ten rounds. To start, do a plebs plank and hold it for 30 seconds. Then, do a squat and hold for another 30 seconds. Hollow Rock Hold for 30 seconds, and repeat. Your transition time will be considered as your resting time.

image.shutterstock.com

70. Cross Training WOD without Equipment # 38: Mime

Do 25 high pull sumo deadlifts and make sure that your form and execution is well done. Repeat this 4 times to complete your WOD.

i.ytimg.com

71. Cross Training WOD without Equipment # 39: High Knee Run

Do 15 seconds' worth of High Knee Runs, then fall into a push up. One push up equals one rep. DO this for five rounds to complete the WOD.

media4.popsugar-assets.com

72. Cross Training WOD without Equipment #40: Simple 1 mile run

Accomplish a one mile run. Do this to your own record time and note your improvements.

beautifulhdwallpaper.com

73. Cross Training WOD without Equipment #41: The Sprint and Walk

Start with a 100 meter sprint. Walk another 100 meters, and repeat for ten rounds.

wallpaperswide.com

74. Cross Training WOD without Equipment #42: The 3 minute handstand

This is simple, really; just put yourself up in a handstand and keep yourself up for three minutes. It's a challenging way to find your balance.

www.lostartofhandbalancing.com

75. *Cross Training WOD without Equipment # 43: Full extension Push Ups*

Put yourself to the test. Do as many push-ups as you can, while keeping your body as straight as possible.

www.wallpaperup.com

76 *Cross Training WOD without Equipment #44: Walking on Your Hands*

This is as challenging as it gets. Do a handstand and attempt to walk that full 100 m. It's okay if you lose your balance. Just keep going until you finish.

i.ytimg.com

77. *Cross Training WOD without Equipment #45: Handstand and Handstand Push Ups*

Balance that Handstand for 30 seconds, and then launch yourself to do five handstand push ups.

wannabewanderer.com

78. *Cross Training WOD without Equipment #46: Tabata Push Ups*

This is mainly for building the upper body strength. Do as many push ups as possible in the span of 20 seconds with a rest of 10 seconds in between. You must do a total of 8 rounds.

i.ytimg.com

79. Cross Training WOD without Equipment #47: Tabata Squats

The same rules apply as with the Tabata Push Ups; only this time, do squats instead.

i.ytimg.com

80. Cross Training WOD without Equipment #48: The High Knee Run AMRAP

Launch yourself in a High Knee Run, ending in a push up after 15 seconds. DO this an AMRAP exercise.

fetch.my

Chapter 4: The Heavy Duty Girls

These Girls are used to build up strength with heavy barbells. Unlike the other Girls, these WODs are used to develop only your strength, and are not mixed with cardio, endurance exercises and the like.

81. Isabel

Isabel will make you do 30 snatches while carrying a weight not less than 135 lbs. Be careful with this one. You may risk injury if you do not pay attention to your form and push it a little too hard.

3.bp.blogspot.com

82.   *Linda*

Linda is done in a 10 – 1 countdown style. First, you must have to deadlift one and a half worth your body weight. Follow this up by benching your body weight. To complete the Linda WOD, Clean 75 % of your body weight.

howtolosebellyfat-forwomen.com

83. Grace

It is recommended that you do this work out with a weight that's right about 135 pounds. You will need 30 cleans, and 30 jerks.

d2ufjv2mjmrw7m.cloudfront.net

Chapter 5: Advanced Cross Training WODs

This chapter may include more difficult exercises, more repetitions, and heavier weights. These are only for the more experienced Cross Training athletes, who developed their strength, agility, endurance and stamina to this level. Observing proper form and caution should be exercised when doing these alone.

84. The Filthy 50

The Filthy 50 is one of the hardest WODs to accomplish. To start, this is a collection of different exercises each done with 50 reps. You do fifty box jumps, fifty jumping pull ups, followed by the same number of kettlebell swings, walking lunge steps, knee to elbow exercises, 45 pound push presses, back extensions, 20 pound wall balls, burpees, then with a jump rope, 50 double unders.

bodyupgradefitness.com

85. The Fran

The Fran is the more difficult version of the invisible Fran. You must accomplish thrusters and pull ups done as fast as you could. Your thrusters must be the maximum weight you can manage. These are done in three rounds, the repetitions done in 21- 15- 9.

www.wallpaperup.com

86. *The Murph*

The Murph is one of the hardest WODs to do with intense exercises and hundreds of reps. Start with a hundred pull ups, followed by two hundred push ups and 300 squats. Run one mile before and after these exercises.

www.gqindia.com

87. The Seven WOD

This involves seven rounds of seven exercises done as quickly as possible. You must do seven handstand pushups followed by the same number of 135-pound thrusters, knee to elbows, 245-pound deadlifts, burpees, kettlebell swings, and finished off by 7 pullups.

88. *The Ryan*

The Ryan involves five rounds of an intense workout. A round consists of seven muscle ups and 21 burpees. These must be done as fast as possible.

i.ytimg.com

89. King Kong

The King Kong is for the heavy lifters only. Deadlift 435 pounds of weight, do two muscle ups, three 250 lbs of squat cleans, followed by four handstand pushups.

timpulvn.ro

90. The Strongman

The Strongman will have you competing against yourself with three rounds of maximum holding. Do an overhead axle hold and hold for your maximum time. Give yourself a three-minute rest and then perform a static crucifix hold for as long as you can then give yourself another three minutes of rest.

www.buntybubly.com

91. Bob's Tasty Combo

Do in repetitions of three and rest as needed. Do five rounds of power cleans and follow up by doing push presses, also in five rounds.

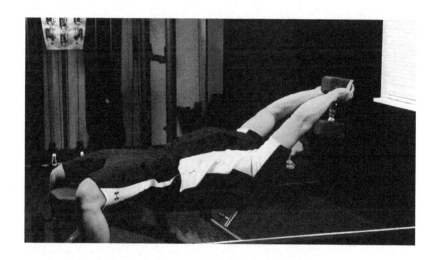

i.ytimg.com

92. *Maximum Load*

Start with deadlifts, with 135 pounds as a minimum weight. Time yourself and continue to your limits.

hdwallpapersfit.com

93. *Turkish Get Ups*

Do Barbell Turkish get ups and work yourself up to 1 RM.

muscleplusfitnessmalaysia.com

94. *Farmer's Carry and Power Cleans*

Accomplish a fifty foot Farmer's carry followed by five rounds of power cleans.

wallpapers-hd-wide.com

95. *Farmers Walk*

Do 70 feet of Farmer's Walk carrying your maximum weight level. Follow this up with 10 burpees. Do this for seven rounds and give yourself a resting time of one minute.

wallpapercave.com

96. The Deadlifts

All of these exercises will involve deadlifts. Begin with two Atlas Stone deadlifts, two Axle deadlifts, two barbell deadlifts and two Farmers handle deadlifts. You can take a rest in between rounds when you need them.

www.google.co.in

97. The Husafell stone carry

Carry your maximum weight and reach for your best distance.

i2.wp.com

98. Swimming WOD

This WOD will require you to do this in 20 minutes, AMRAP. Do a 50 m swim followed by 25 push ups, 25 squats, and 25 double unders with your jump rope.

wall.alphacoders.com

99. Swimming WOD #2

Perform three rounds of a 200 meter backstroke, followed by 20 double snatches and finished off by 35 push ups.

wall.alphacoders.com

100. Swimming WOD #3

This WOD is started by a 50 meter swim, followed by 15 wall balls and 15 push ups, and is repeated for six rounds.

wall.alphacoders.com

Conclusion

These Cross Training exercises can lead you to the body you can only have dreamed of otherwise. Follow the instructions and pay attention to the proper placement of your body for optimal results. Work your way to a fitter, stronger and healthier you. You are guaranteed to see great results very soon.

Do this according to your own pace. If you do your exercises faithfully, your Cross Training skills will enhance greatly, and you'll have the body to prove it too.

Finally, if you enjoyed this book, please take the time to share your thoughts and post a positive review on Amazon. It'd be greatly appreciated!

Thank you and good luck!

Made in the USA
Coppell, TX
06 December 2021

67343783R00066